MY COMMISSIONS.

NEW YORK:
LATIMER BROS. & SEYMOUR, PRINTERS, 21 NASSAU STREET.

1860.

When the New York and Erie Railroad was finished to Dunkirk, though traversing the entire southern tier of counties of this State, waking the echoes of that sequestered region to the scream of the locomotive and the thunder of its ponderous train, the great *idea* which originated its construction was by no means fully developed. The West, with its increasing abundance and its millions of people, lay away beyond this terminus. True, its connections reached through Ohio and the States of the West, but those connections were attended with great inconveniences, and were made at points which failed to develope all the capabilities of this great artery of trade and travel. The gauge of the Erie was broad—that of the roads with which it was connected was narrow. Hence the necessity that not only passengers should change cars, but that every pound of freight should be transferred at Dunkirk, in order to reach a market over the Erie road. Besides these disadvantages, a glance at the map will show that Dunkirk is out of the line of direct communication with the principal centres of travel of the West. Cincinnati and St. Louis, the two chief points aimed at by the construction of the New York and Erie Railroad, lie far south of a line running from New York through Dunkirk; and while it was deemed important to reach Lake Erie at that point, yet that was regarded rather as an incident than as the main object to be attained. The New York Central almost monopolized the railway traffic directly west of Dunkirk, and Buffalo controlled, to a large extent, the traffic of the lake. To meet these exigencies, the grand idea was to furnish, in almost a direct line, a continuous track, on a broad gauge, from New York to Cincinnati, and from thence to St. Louis. While the New York and Erie was being constructed, a road on a broad gauge was completed between the two latter cities, and the great thing then to be accomplished was to push the New York and Erie, with its broad gauge, forward to Cincinnati, thus enabling the passenger who started from the Hudson river to go through to that city, or even to St. Louis, without the inconvenience of change. The vessel, too, that drew up by the side of the railroad dock, opposite New York, could discharge her cargo destined to the West into a train that should carry it without change, and without breaking bulk, to St. Louis, delivering it, as it was received from the ship, into the store-houses there, or upon the steamers that ply on the Mississippi. To carry out this grand idea, the States of New York, Pennsylvania, and Ohio chartered the Atlantic and Great Western Railway Company, for the purpose of constructing a road connecting with the Erie at Little Valley, in this State, and terminating at Dayton, in Ohio. Though included in three separate charters, and lying in part in three different States, yet this is, in fact, one corporation, and managed by a single direction. From Dayton to Cincinnati a railway has already been constructed, on which a third rail was about being laid, which would make the connection perfect.

The Atlantic and Great Western Railway Company had been thus chartered. A company of wealthy gentlemen had taken the contract to build and equip the road. They were to receive a certain percentage of their pay in cash, and a certain other percentage in the mortgage bonds and certificates of paid up shares, to be issued as the work progressed. Under this arrangement a portion of the work had been done, when it was brought to a sudden stop from the lack of funds to carry it on. This stoppage occurred about the latter part of the year 1856; a year which, with the one that followed it, will long be remembered as the most disastrous to railway enterprises that had ever occurred in this country. Railway shares had depreciated all over the world, railway bonds had become a drug in every market, and railway contractors were suspending or becoming bankrupt everywhere.

It was at this unfortunate juncture that my financial connection with the Atlantic and Great Western Railway commenced; a connection which, while it resulted in the realization by the company and the contractors of the means of completing their road, has been a source of vast expense and infinite vexation to me. I do not specially complain of this. I am seeking no man's sympathy. I have seen enough of the world to know that fortunes are not to be made without some trouble and much vexation, and I am prepared to encounter my share of these. But I found that road bankrupt in money and in credit, utterly unable to move one foot towards the completion of a work so patriotically begun. I placed it upon a solid basis. It was my energy and my agency that infused renewed vitality into it, and I had a right to expect that when I had done all this I should be awarded and permitted to receive so much, at least, as had been solemnly promised me by those whose fortunes I had saved from wreck. My purpose now is to give to the stockholders of the company, and all who feel an interest in the enterprise they have undertaken, a history containing the simple truth as to what I have done in relatian to their road, what I claim, and demonstrating that I am, in equity and good faith, by every principle of fair dealing and common honesty between man and man, entitled to what I am compelled to seek through the coercive instrumentalities of the Courts.

I said the contractors, Messrs. Henry Doolittle and A. C. Morton, had agreed to finish and equip the road, and to receive in part payment a large amount of the mortgage bonds of the company and certificates of paid up shares. The money they were to receive, or, at all events, so far as the company were able to pay it, had been expended; and they had as yet no iron, and no part of the necessary equipments of the road, and no means of purchasing them, save the bonds and stock of the company. To enable them to go on to the completion of their contract, they required thirty-one thousand tons of rails, and a present amount nearly equal to a million of dollars in money. Without these it was folly to think of going on at all. To obtain these in this country was, in their position, utterly out of the question. The iron was not here, or if it was, it was beyond their ability to purchase it with the means at their command. The capital was not here, or what was eqally fatal to them, confidence in railway securities had become so impaired, and facilities for more profitable investments were so abundant, as to render the borrowing of a million of money on railway securities, among our own people, a simple impossibility. Hence it became necessary that an agent should be employed to go abroad, to endeavor, at least, to effect what it was impossible to accomplish here. I was applied to as that agent. I had had some experience in negotiations of this kind, and the result will bear me out in saying that those who made the application had a just appreciation of my capabilities in that respect. The undertaking all conceded to be a doubtful one, and at best involving an outlay of much time and large expense. In view of these facts, I hesitated to accept the position tendered me on any terms. My own business required my attention; the sacrifice of time and money would be great, and without a promise of compensation, if successful, commensurate with the chances of loss by failure, I refused to leave my business and my home at all. But the company, as well as the contractors, were in a dilemma. The former had expended all their corporate funds, and were unable, for the present, to procure more, and the latter were absolutely compelled to suspend work from lack of means to go on. They had not the experience, nor, I may be permitted to say, the financial tact to carry a negotiation of such magnitude forward to a successful termination. They were urgent in their appeals for my services, and lavish in promises of compensation, and I consented to go abroad, but I refused to enter into any positive agreement until I had visited Europe and ascertained whether there was a hope of eventual success, though the *basis* of an agreement was fixed upon in case I should undertake the negotiation. I accordingly went to Europe at my own expense. Soon after my arrival in London I was joined by the contractors, Messrs. Doolittle and Morton. They had ample powers from the company to do everything, to make any contract necessary to carry out the objects of the negotiation, and effectuate the purchase of the iron, and the loan of the money. Besides, they held, or would be entitled to receive, the bonds and stock of the company to an amount sufficient to carry out any reasonable contract they might make in reference to those objects.

After some time spent in England, I entered into an agreement with Messrs. Doolittle & Morton, by which I undertook to negotiate a loan for them of £193,000 sterling, and also the purchase of 31,000 tons of rails. This loan and purchase of rails were to be based mainly upon the security (as collateral) of the first mortgage bonds of the company. This contract was a verbal one, but was in substance the same as that which was subsequently reduced to writing, which will be mentioned in the order of events, and which will be found in my appendix marked "C." If the compensation secured to me by that contract seems large, it will be remembered that I had left a prosperous and successful business at home ;—that I had undertaken a work that might occupy years, and which actually did occupy about two years of my time abroad ;—that the bonds and stock in which I was to be paid, had, as yet, no fixed or permanent commercial value in the market. True, I regarded them as valuable, but there were those who did not regard the stock or the bonds of the road as of any positive or certain value. It will be remembered, too, that I might, after all, wholly fail to effect any loan of money or purchase of iron, in which case my time, my expenses, and all the vexation and mortification of failure would be my own undivided loss. It was, therefore, a mere matter of judgment on my part, a matter of uncertain speculation whether I should be successful at all; and if so, whether I should, in fact, receive more than sufficient to compensate me for the hazards and positive losses I was sure to encounter. Be all this as it may, the agreement was consummated, and I entered upon the task of loaning the money and purchasing the iron.

I knew the labor that was before me, and I fortified myself accordingly. I procured letters from the best and most distinguished men of the States, testifying to my respectability as a citizen and a business man. Among those to whom I was thus indebted are United States Senators, members of Congress, Governors of States, and members of the National Cabinet—some of whose letters will be found in my appendix. If they were complimentary, I must be pardoned for saying that they are also just. They said the truth of me then. They are true of me still. The generous kindness of the writers was never abused, either in Europe or this country, by me; and it will be remembered with gratitude while I live. In order to facilitate the business as far as possible, I associated with me a gentleman of high social and financial position in London, one who had access to commercial circles and capitalists of Europe, and through whose aid I could gain a proper introduction in the proper quarters.

Those who have experienced the difficulty of negotiating loans among the capitalists of Europe on American securities, other than United States or State stocks, will appreciate the difficulties which were encountered in this case. Most of the capitalists would not listen to us at all. Others heard us coldly and read us in reply long homilies on the stringency of the times, the uncertainty of railroad enterprises, and the doubtful credit of American securities generally. Others again gave us a patient audience, and encouraged our expectations ; but days and weeks, and months wore on, while we suffered the anxieties of hope deferred, to be wholly disappointed at last. Thus we labored from February until September, always busy with the moneyed men of Europe, explaining the capabilities and prospects of our road, demonstrating its merits and the certainty of the solid value of the securities we offered, before we found a capitalist of sufficient courage to invest his money on the credit of our representations and our bonds. On the 30th of September, A.D. 1857, we succeeded in perfecting a contract for a loan of £193,000 sterling, with Mr. Henry Gompertz, a gentleman of the city of London. This agreement (which will be found in my appendix marked A) was certainly liberal in its terms towards Mr. Gompertz, and we call the reader's attention to those terms, for they allowed him a very wide margin for profits ; but it was satisfactory to the other parties, and they were content with its provisions. It will be seen, by a reference to the agreement, that the money was to be advanced by instalments on the drafts of Messrs. Doolittle & Morton, drawn upon and accepted by the banking house of Samuel Hallett & Co , of which house I was the principal, secured by a deposit of the first mortgage bonds to the amounts provided for by the contract, with Benjamin Moran, Esq., of London, who was appointed a trustee for that purpose.

Thus, after eight months of anxious and earnest negotiation, an agreement for the required amount of money was consummated, and that part of my mission seemed to be accomplished. Mr. Gompertz, through his own means and his commercial associations, was supposed to be abundantly able to carry out his undertakings, and it now remained only to effect the purchase of the 31,000 tons of rails in order to complete the business that carried me to Europe and enable the Atlantic and Great Western Railway Company to finish the enterprise upon which it had entered.

Negotiations for that purpose were opened with various iron manufacturers and iron merchants in England and on the continent, all of which ultimately failed. At length an arrangement was effected with Mr. Henry Gompertz, the same gentleman who had agreed to furnish the money, to furnish the rails also; and on the 30th of October he entered into a contract to furnish 31,000 tons of rails, upon the terms and conditions stated therein. This contract, too, was liberal in its terms towards Mr. Gompertz, allowing him a liberal margin for profits. But, like the other, it was satisfactory to the parties interested, and we of course were content. By this agreement, which will be found in the appendix marked B, it will be seen that the rails were to be delivered by instalments on board of vessels at Liverpool, and were to be paid for by drafts drawn by Messrs. Doolittle & Morton, upon and accepted by Samuel Hallett & Co., and secured by deposits with Benjamin Moran, Esq., the same trustee named in the first contract, of first mortgage bonds of the company, to the amount and in the manner specified in the agreement. I repeat that the terms of this purchase were certainly liberal towards Mr. Gompertz, affording a very broad margin for profits. But Messrs. Doolittle & Morton regarded their interests as largely subserved by the arrangement, and it was for them and the company to ratify and confirm it. This they did.

Up to this time the compensation which I was to receive for effectuating the loan and purchasing the iron rested in parol, or in correspondence passing between my employers and myself. But affairs had now arrived at a crisis when the whole business appeared to be on the eve of completion, and it was necessary that our agreement should also be reduced to writing and properly executed. Accordingly the contract, of which Exhibit C is a copy, was duly entered into between Messrs. Doolittle & Morton and myself.

It is proper, in reference to my compensation as provided for in this contract, that I should remark here that whoever supposes negotiations of this magnitude can be carried on in Europe without a large outlay of money and a division to some extent of commissions, makes a very grave mistake; and it is but simple justice to myself to say, that when the fact was accomplished, that portion of my compensation to be ultimately appropriated to myself had been greatly reduced.

I said I had associated with myself a gentleman of high standing, socially and commercially, in the negotiations for obtaining the money and the iron. I allude to John Goddard, Esquire, of London, who was actuary of the Rock Life Insurance Company, one of the richest institutions of London. Although a cloud seems to have drifted between us,—how or from what quarter I certainly cannot imagine,—yet, I will do him the justice to say that he is one of the noblest and most honorable men I have ever known—one who comes up, in every respect, to the true standard of the English gentleman—and that in the management of this affair, as well as in many other respects, I am under obligations to him which I shall remember with gratitude always. To compensate him and his associates for his and their services, Messrs. Doolittle & Morton entered into an agreement with him, a copy of which will be found in the appendix, marked D. Whether his compensation as provided for in the agreement, is too much or too little, is a matter in relation to which I have nothing to say. It was satisfactory to the parties, and being so, I have neither the right nor the disposition to find fault.

These contracts having all been completed, the parties to which seemed to be perfectly able and willing to perform their covenants, the business appeared to be, in the main, closed, and the principal mission which originally sent me to Europe accomplished. I had effectuated a loan of the requisite amount of money, and a purchase of the iron necessary to complete the road in a manner satisfactory to the parties in whose interest I had been employed. They had adopted and entered into agreements which I had negotiated, thereby ratifying and confirming my acts, and it remained only for me to accept the drafts of Messrs. Doolittle & Morton, as drawn, and my labors would be completed. I had earned, and would be entitled to my commissions as they became due under the contract, and this would have ended my connection with the financial affairs of the contractors and the Atlantic and Great Western R. R. Co.

Of the drafts provided for in the contract with Mr. Gompertz, the amount of £217,000, in the sums and payable in the manner provided in the contracts (A and B), were drawn by Messrs. Doolittle & Morton upon, and were accepted by Samuel Hallett & Co., and which, with the requisite and corresponding amount of bonds, were deposited with Benjamin Moran, Esq., the trustee, in part performance of the contract on their part. Notice of such deposit was duly given by the trustee to Mr. Gompertz, a copy of which notice will be found in the appendix, marked F. By this deposit Messrs. Doolittle & Morton had done all they were required to do until after Mr. Gompertz had entered upon the performance of his part of the contracts, and thus the whole matter seemed to be closed.

But the commercial revulsions of the fall and winter of 1857–8 threw financial matters all over the world into utter confusion. Capitalists everywhere were toppling down, or were paralyzed by the chaos of the times ;—banks suspended specie payments, debts remained unpaid, and contracts were everywhere unfulfilled. In anticipation of the performance of the agreements by Mr. Gompertz, the contractors, Messrs. Doolittle & Morton, had made arrangements which would be disastrous to them, in case of his failure to keep his engagements. In view of these facts, and of the uncertainty which hung around all commercial transactions, and to secure, as far as human agencies could do so, against any failure in the supply of money and iron, as provided for in Mr. Gompertz' undertakings, a contract was entered into on the 13th Nov. 1857, between Messrs. Doolittle & Morton, of the one part, and John Goddard, Esq., and Samuel Hallett & Co., of the other part, which will be found in the appendix, marked E. It will be seen by the contract that we undertook to guarantee performance on the part of Mr. Gompertz of the covenants entered into by him to furnish the money and the iron, according to the terms and upon the conditions of his agreements ;—that if he failed, we were to step into his place, do, or cause to be done, what he was to do, and be paid the amount, including bonus and commissions that he was to be paid. For undertaking this guarantee, we were to be paid the amount stipulated in the contract E. This, of course, involved a necessity for my remaining in Europe. Neither Mr. Goddard nor myself were able, from our own means, to perform all that Mr. Gompertz had agreed to perform, in case of his failure ; but our position was such, that, with the additional commissions allowed us, bad as the times were, that we could procure other parties to step in and aid us in furnishing the funds and the iron according to the terms of our undertaking. This the parties understood, and I submit that the facts which transpired subsequently demonstrate that they were not mistaken.

In the confidence that the business was now satisfactorily arranged, and that the money and the iron would be forthcoming at the proper time, Messrs. Doolittle & Morton returned to America to perfect their arrangements for resuming work on their road early in the spring.

Thus matters stood until February, 1858. In the meantime, the financial difficulties in America culminated in the ruin of thousands of houses regarded as the strongest and firmest in the country. Banks were driven to a suspension of specie payments ; mercantile credit was for the time annihilated, and universal distrust pervaded alike city and country. Among the things that suffered most were railway securities. Stocks ran down and down till many classes disappeared into the abyss that yawns beneath the financial cypher ; others that had been regarded as solid almost as gold, went down to 80, to 70, to 60, with scarcely a hope of limit to their downward course. Railway bonds shared the common destiny. They, too, went down and down till all faith in their solidarity appeared to be gone. Stockholders, as they saw their investments vanishing away beneath the pressure of the times, denounced every railway scheme as a gigantic swindle ;—bondholders execrated what they were pleased to term the knavery of railway management, till odium—infamy almost—as well as supposed worthlessness in money value, attached alike to scrip and bonds.

The commercial storm swept across the Atlantic with a fury almost as desolating as it had exhibited in this country. Mercantile and manufacturing houses were swept down before it. The Scotch banks exploded. Even the strongest American banking house in London was compelled to borrow a million of pounds sterling to avoid a necessity of suspension, and thus the same financial chaos that ruled in this country prevailed to a large extent there. There, too, as in this country, American railway securities, more than any other kind of property, felt the disastrous influence of the times. The panic, in regard to commercial credit, was intensified a hundred-fold in relation to them. The press of England opened upon them. The London *Times*, the paper having the largest circulation and mightiest influence of any in Europe, whose approval is commercial life, and whose censure is commercial death, thundered against them. The smaller papers took up the cry, and echoed it, until it was regarded as almost an insult to offer a British capitalist a railway bond at any price.

Such was the condition of things when, as the time of performance approached, it became evident that Mr. Gompertz would not be able to perform his agreements. In times like those of the winter of 1857–'58, scarcely an individual in Europe could command of his own in actual cash for investment, a million of dollars, and there was small hope of borrowing it upon individual credit until the times should mend, and commercial confidence be restored. The fear of the failure of Mr. Gompertz to perform his contracts ripened into certainty, and it became evident that negotiations must be opened anew. The reasons for such failure need not be discussed here. Who was to blame, or whether blame should attach anywhere other than to the disasters of the times, it is bootless to inquire. It was bad enough to know that a year of vexation and anxiety such as no amount of compensation would induce me again to undergo, propitious as its close seemed to have been, was entirely lost. Still Mr. Goddard and myself had guaranteed that the money and the iron to finish the Atlantic and Great Western Railway should be furnished, and it became our duty and our highest interest to see that our covenants should not be broken. We, of course, could not of ourselves furnish the means to fulfil the contracts of Mr. Gompertz, nor was our personal credit equal to securing the requisite amount, but we had a position which gave us access to capitalists, and characters which entitled us to their respect. We had, moreover, under our contract of guarantee a large bonus which enabled us to offer, though at the sacrifice of our own interests, superior inducements to tempt capitalists to come to our aid. Besides, we had the benefit of the contracts with Mr. Gompertz, which were very advantageous. Their terms were most liberal, and had he been able to have carried them out, would have realized a fortune with which most people would have been contented from the profits of them. These considerations, notwithstanding the terrible nature of the times, gave us encouragement, and we entered upon our new negotiations for the money and the rails by no means without confidence in their results. We were not disappointed.

Mr. Gompertz failed to perform his contracts, and notice was served upon us, (Goddard & Hallett,) a copy of which will be found in the appendix, marked F F, requiring us to go on and perform our covenants, guaranteeing performance of the conditions of the Gompertz contracts. We were thus required to raise £193,000 sterling in money, and to furnish 31,000 tons of rails upon the same terms and conditions, and according to the stipulations contained in those contracts. In other words, we were to step into the place of Mr. Gompertz, do all that he was to do, and receive all that he was to receive by way of payment, commissions, and bonus. We immediately set about the accomplishment of the gigantic labor that was before us, and that, too, at the very worst possible time for us. I visited Germany and France and other portions of the continent in pursuit of capitalists with whom to negotiate a loan of the money, while Mr. Goddard plied himself earnestly and industriously in England. I negotiated a loan of the Bank of Switzerland, the contract for which was duly executed, a copy of which will be found in the appendix, marked G. This contract, from causes not necessary to be mentioned here, was subsequently, by mutual consent, rescinded. I perfected an arrangement with the *Credit Mobiler*, of Paris, to furnish one-half of all the amount necessary, and a contract to that effect was duly executed, a copy of which will be found in the appendix, marked H. This, too, was subsequently, by mutual consent, rescinded, for causes which need not be stated now. I refer to these facts only to show the diligence with which I plied myself to the performance of our agreements.

On the 13th of February, 1858, we perfected a contract with R. W. Kennard & Co., of London, for a loan of £135,000 sterling. This contract was duly executed on that day, and will be found in the appendix, marked I. Soon after, we perfected a contract with Leon Lillo & Co., bankers, of Paris and Salamanca, for the loan of £200,000 sterling. A copy of this contract will be found in the appendix, marked J. On the 23d day of April, 1858, we perfected a contract for the purchase of 15,500 tons of rails with the Ebbu Vale Iron Company, which contract will be found in the appendix, marked K. And on the same day we perfected a contract with Bailey Brothers, of Liverpool, for the purchase of 15,500 tons of rails, which contract will be found in the appendix, marked L. By these two latter contracts it will be seen that we agreed for the purchase of thirty-one thousand tons of rails, which was to be paid for, half in money or bankers' bills, and half in the mortgage bonds of the company, at a rate stipulated therein. This was a departure from the letter of the contracts with Mr. Gompertz, but it will be seen that by the two former agreements (I and J) a sufficient amount of money was provided to pay for the one-half of the rails, and leave a balance of £193,000 sterling, and a small margin to cover interest. Besides, we had the direct sanction and consent of Messrs. Doolittle & Morton and the company for such departure, and our contracts were subsequently ratified and adopted by them.

These four contracts being with parties abundantly able to perform them, and being, moreover, on terms quite as favorable as those offered by Mr. Gompertz, the main part of our labor was accomplished, and it remained only for those in whose behalf we acted to approve and accept them in performance of our covenants, and my mission would be at an end. Messrs. Doolittle & Morton were in America, and the persons with whom we had contracted to furnish the money and the iron required their sanction and approval, as also that of the Atlantic and Great Western Railway Company, of the agreements we had made. I wrote to Messrs. Doolittle & Morton, inclosing them copies of the contracts, and requesting them to come over to Europe for the purpose of ratifying and carrying them out; and also to bring some authorized agent of the company, or be empowèred anew themselves to act for the company in approving and sanctioning them. A copy of this letter will be found in the appendix, marked O. The reply of Mr. Doolittle will be found in the appendix, marked P.

On the 26th day of May, 1858, Mr. Doolittle, who was now the sole representative of the firm of Doolittle & Morton, the latter having retired from it, arrived in Europe. He was accompanied by C. L. Ward, Esq., the President of the Atlantic and Great Western Railway. On their arrival at Bremen they telegraphed me at London to meet them at Paris. I went to Paris, accompanied by Thomas W. Kennard, Esq., one of the firm of R. W. Kennard & Co., the firm with whom I had contracted for a loan of £135,000. (*Vide* Appendix, I.) I met Messrs. Doolittle & Ward at Paris, and there after personal consultation, and after being made perfectly acquainted with our doings, they fully ratified, approved, and adopted the contract made with

Leon Lillo & Co. (*Vide* Appendix.) They then accompanied me to London and had an interview with the iron masters, Messrs. Bailey, Brothers & Co., and the Ebbu Vale Iron Company, the parties with whom I had contracted for the rails (see Appendix, K and L), and those contracts were fully ratified and adopted by them. They also ratified, confirmed, and adopted the contract made with R. W. Kennard & Co. for the advance of £135,000. (*Vide* Appendix, I.)

The parties to these contracts were all responsible, abundantly able to perform their undertakings. They had bound themselves to do all that Mr. Gompertz had covenanted to do, on terms as favorable to the company and to Messrs. Doolittle & Morton, as those contained in his contracts. The contracts made by us (Goddard & Hallett) having been ratified, confirmed, and adopted by those for whom we acted, and parties thus solvent and satisfactory to our principals, accepted in our stead by them, we, as a legal as well as a logical sequence, had performed our agreement, and were discharged from its provisions. Having performed our covenants to the satisfaction of our covenanters, we were entitled to our pay.

Thus my mission of negotiating the means to complete the Atlantic and Great Western Railway was a second time accomplished, and what was peculiarly satisfactory was the fact that it now rested upon a basis believed to be solid, and which subsequent developments have proved it to be entirely so. These contracts and modifications of them negotiated by me, and executed by me, are the only contracts under which the iron and money for the construction have thus far been furnished, and under which the money and the iron are now from time to time furnished. This is the best evidence that they were satisfactory, and surely no one will doubt that they have been sanctioned and adopted. It is the highest proof of approval of my acts, and had I failed (as I certainly have not) to preserve the written record of approval of every step I took from the beginning of these negotiations an equivalent, for such record would be found here. It would, then, seem that it only remained for me to receive the compensation which my contracts gave me, and thus terminate my connection with the affairs of the road. But the amount of that compensation was large. It was to be paid in installments in proportion to, and as the various amounts were realized by the contractors of the road. I repeat, the amount of my compensation was large (how large will appear by the statement in my appendix), and now that my labors are completed, the difficulties having been removed out of the way of the company, and the contractors, and every thing working smoothly with them, the magnitude of the commissions and compensations they had agreed to pay me seemed to appal them. They had not the manhood to come square up to their agreements and pay my covenanted amounts, nor had they the hardihood to deny their agreements and shirk payment altogether. They forgot that I had neglected my business at home almost to its absolute ruin: they forgot that I had taken up my residence abroad, in their service, for two years: they forgot that I had expended, by way of counsel fees, travelling expenses, sub-commissions and agencies, more than $50,000 in money, and that I had never received one dollar from them. All these considerations they forgot or overlooked in contemplating what they were pleased to term the enormous amount of my compensation. Hence began a series of evasions, more vexatious, if possible, than the previous negotiations, and which threaten to be quite as interminable. True the work I had undertaken to do had been done to their satisfaction. There was no complaint on that score. The means to carry on the work to completion had been provided, and were continually coming forward. The contractors were saved from bankruptcy and the managers of the road from dishonor, but my commissions were large, and my employers, repenting of their liberality in promises while I was lifting them out of their troubles, now that they were at ease determined that those commissionsshould be reduced, whatever cost of principle and good faith it might involve. I was anxious to retire from the business in Europe and return home. I was wearied with the vexations and delays which had occurred from the beginning, and to which I saw but a faint prospect of termination. I therefore entered into an agreement with Mr. Doolittle and the president of the company to assign the contracts with the parties who were to furnish the money, and the rails (*vide* Appendix, I, J, K, L) to Mr. James McHenry, of Liverpool, for the benefit of all concerned. He had previously purchased all the interest of Mr. Goddard, who was to retire from the business when paid. As preliminary to such assignment, Mr. McHenry entered into a contract with Mr. Doolittle, embracing in substance the contract of guarantee between Mr. Goddard and myself, and Messrs. Doolittle & Morton. (A copy of this contract will be found in the appendix, marked 2.) He also delivered to me a declaration that such contract was entered into by him in trust for himself and me, and that I was entitled to the half of the bonus and Commissions which he was to receive under such contract. (A copy of this declaration will be found in the appendix, marked R.) These papers having been duly executed, I assigned, by the direction of Mr. Doolittle and the president of the company, the four contracts to Mr. McHenry. This transfer was made to enable Mr. McHenry to carry out his agreement with Mr. Doolittle (Appendix, 2) to furnish the money and iron and to provide for the payment of my compensation, beyond the amount stipulated for in my first contract with Doolittle & Morton. (Appendix, C.)

Here my connection with the financial affairs of the company was in fact closed, so far as the raising of money and means to complete the road was concerned. I had not as yet received a dollar from any person connected with it. My own affairs at home had from neglect, on my part, become embarassed. It needed all my energies to prevent my own bankruptcy. I thought I could look forward with certainty to relief, when the time of payment of my commissions and compensation, which seemed to be made secure through the McHenry contracts (Appendix, 2 and R), should come around—I anticipated no trouble. I had already, for the sake of prompt and certain liquidation, surrendered half of what I was legally entitled to demand under my sealed covenants; and I had a right to suppose that those for whom I had sacrificed so much, would now, at least, in the performance of their agreements with me, take care of my interests, as I, in fulfilling my covenants with them, had taken care of theirs. I rested, therefore, easy in the faith that troubles of the present would give place to calm and quiet in a proximate future—that, dark as to-day might be, there would be brightness again to-morrow. In all this I was to be disappointed. The magnitude of the bonus secured by the contract with Mr. Doolittle (Appendix, 2) dazzled the vision of Mr. McHenry, and from the moment of the execution of that contract, all the energies of his mind appeared to be bent upon the purpose of securing the whole of it to himself, instead of a division with me, according to the arrangement between the parties and his express agreement, with me, as contained in his declaration of trust. (Appendix, R.) I will not stop here to detail the petty vexations and annoyances to which I was subjected. They were such as made the "head sick and the heart faint." Disgusted with the bad faith and ingratitude of those whom I had served, whose fortunes I had saved, or made, and threatened with embarrassments and ruin at home, I was prepared to make almost any sacrifice to be rid of the whole affair, which should not leave me absolutely a bankrupt in fortune or reputation. It will be seen by a careful reading of the various contracts referred to, that I had already, as I have said, surrendered more than half my stipulated compensation—an amount that would be regarded by most men as of itself a princely fortune—and I was prepared, for the sake of quiet, and of being relieved from a matter productive, to me at least, only of vexation from the beginning, to make a further sacrifice of the half of what still justly and legally remained to me. I therefore made to Mr. McHenry, as a last and final proposition—one that should end all cavil and all dispute between us,—the offer to receive of him, in satisfaction of our contract, the one-half of what, by the well-defined and well-understood terms of our agreements (Appendix, 2 and R), I was fairly and legally entitled to have. This proposition was accepted by Mr. McHenry, and it was arranged that the amount, being one quarter of the bonus given in his contract with Mr. Doolittle (Appendix, 2), should be paid to me as follows: three-fourths in the mortgage bonds of the company, and the remaining fourth in paid up shares of the stock, to be paid as the bonds and stock should come into his hands under his contract with Mr. Doolittle and the company. In pursuance of this agreement, five several drafts were drawn by me upon, and accepted by Mr. McHenry, amounting in the aggregate to the sum I was to receive, copies of which are given in the appendix marked S. Upon the acceptance of these drafts I surrendered up to him his agreement with me, and gave him a discharge from all liability, save from the drafts themselves.

Here again the matter seemed to have been brought to a close, and all chance for difficulty or vexation ended. I arranged my affairs to return home, in the comfortable faith that in due time I should receive the amount of the acceptances, in the manner and at the times provided, which, while it would not make me rich, would relieve me from embarrassments that had grown up during my absence, and leave me at least an amount of commercial credit that would enable me to go on with my legitimate business without impeachment of my solvency, or that of my house. In this faith I returned to the United States, but in this I was not permitted long to rest.

On my arrival at home I found myself embarrassed. I found a larger amount of liabilities than I had the immediate ability to discharge, but in these acceptances of Mr. McHenry, and my right to the bonds on which they were based, I had the means of present security and ultimate liquidation, with a large margin to spare. This indebtedness grew out of endorsements for railroad contractors, against which I supposed I was amply secured, but contractors and securities had gone down together, involving me to some extent in their fall. To secure my creditors and relieve myself from embarrassment, I turned out to them a portion of the McHenry drafts, and they were sent forward for liquidation in the manner provided by them. To my utter astonishment Mr. M'Henry refused to pay, or respond in any manner recognizing their validity as against him. I wrote him again and again, but could get no answer. He was in possession of bonds and stock sufficient for the discharge of the drafts sent forward,—bonds and stock received by him for the purpose of paying them, but he happened to think that the ocean which rolled between us was at once a bar to any coercive measures against him, and a release from those obligations of good faith which honorable men hold sacred. I sent an agent to England to endeavor to effect a settlement with him. After months of delay, my agent returned, having effected nothing. Mr. Doolittle, knowing my rights, and the justice as well as legality of my claims, and, moreover, supposing himself to be in a position to influence Mr. McHenry to do right in the matter, undertook to negotiate a settlement between us.

As preliminary to a settlement, it was insisted that my creditors and myself should invest, in the first mortgage bonds of the Atlantic and Great Western Railway Company, an amoun of money equal to twenty per cent. of the amount of the McHenry acceptances which were held by us—that is to say, Mr. McHenry demanded, as a consideration for his performance of his agreements with me, that we should advance, towards the construction of the road, an amount of money equal to twenty per cent. of his acceptances, for which we were to receive the first mortgage bonds of the company at seventy-five cents on the dollar. There were other stipulations connected with this proposition, which will be found in the contract subsequently entered into. This proposition was accepted, but on the eve of its being reduced to the form of a mutual agreement, it was withdrawn. It was then insisted that the percentage of money to be advanced should be forty per cent! Monstrous as this proposition was, when considered with reference to all the principles of honorable dealing, it was accepted. There was no danger of ultimate loss to the parties advancing the money, for the bonds would be ample security when the road should be constructed, and I was anxious to aid, as far as I could, its completion. Besides, it was desirable that capitalists in this country should invest somewhat in the enterprise, thus testifying their confidence in its merits, and, therefore, much as we were shocked at that laxity of commercial honor which requires a bonus by way of inducement to the performance of its covenants, we submitted to the exaction. Accordingly on the 28th day of October, 1859, a contract was entered into between Mr. McHenry and myself, through our respective agents, embodying the terms of this new settlement, a copy of which, with the modifications, will be found in the appendix, marked T.

It was now supposed that a perfect settlement had been effected, and that no further difficulty could possibly arise. We, therefore, entered earnestly, and in a spirit of good faith, upon the performance of our undertakings. Provision for raising and paying the money was made, and a portion of the money advanced, according to the terms and conditions, and at the times stated in the contracts and the modifications thereof. In seeming performance of his part of the agreement, Mr. McHenry deposited the bonds, as provided in the contract, with various banks, and other depositories, in the city of New York and elsewhere.

It will be noted that we were entitled to receive under the contract, as modified, a portion of our pay in the bonds of that portion of the road lying in the State of New York, on which portion the money advanced by us was required to be expended. The importance attached to our having the New York bonds will be appreciated, when it is understood that the money to be advanced by us, was by the contract to be expended in New York, was to be paid in instalments as the work progressed, and was not all to be paid until the rails were laid. It will be remembered, also, that the money received from Europe had thus far been expended in New York, carrying the road forward from the New York terminus, and completing it as the work advanced. The iron was used in New York. The persons in Europe advancing the money and iron, received the Ohio and Pennsylvania bonds in proportion to the length of the road in each of these States. Suppose, then, that when the road should be finished to the Pennsylvania line, the supply of money and iron were to fail, and the work stop: we would (in the absence of the New York bonds) have bonds covering no actuality, but only an imaginary railway, valueless as the paper on which they were written. We, therefore, as the money was advanced, called for the New York bonds, as provided for in the modified contract. These were promised from time to time, as we paid our own money, but delivery was, under various pretences, evaded, until at last Mr. McHenry absolutely refused to deliver us any of the New York bonds at all.

This, of course, brought everything to a sudden stop again,

and it remained only for me to place myself in such a position that I could not be made to suffer by any lack of good faith or delay of performance on the part of Mr. McHenry. I tendered, in a legal form, performance on my part, and demanded of Mr. McHenry performance on his. I demanded the portion of New York bonds to which I was entitled. These were refused, and this contract of settlement, like every one that had preceded it, vanished into air.

Further negotiations with a party who held no faith with me would be idle, and I availed myself of the last and only resort for a final adjustment of my claims. I appealed to the law. I filed a bill in equity against Mr. McHenry, asking a decree for specific performance of his contract with me. I procured an injunction restraining the removal of the bonds from the hands of the various depositories, until the final adjudication of the courts on the subject of my claims shall be made.

I have been forced into this litigation against my best exertion, and against my will. I have made such sacrifices as few men would have made to avoid it. I should be heartily glad to avoid it now; but if I must, in search of an adjustment of my claims, travel through the courts, be it so. It will not ruin or greatly embarrass me. I am content to bide my time, and the action of the tribunals of justice. I have the patience to endure, and the means of carrying forward this litigation, if need be, to the bitter end. But I tell the stockholders, and present owners of the bonds of the Atlantic and Great Western Railway, the value of whose shares and bonds depend upon the completion of their road, and I tell the contractors whose fortunes depend upon the continued supply of the means to carry on the work, that they cannot afford in such perilous times, to let this controversy ripen into litigation with the company. I tell the managers of the road, past and present, that they cannot afford, in the very commencement of their enterprise, to lead off in an interminable war in the courts at law. I do not say this in bravado, nor by way of threat, but as a simple truth growing out of the peculiarities of my position, and which, if this litigation goes on, must become public history.

I have felt a deep interest in this enterprise ever since it was first originated. I regarded it as an integral part of a great system, of which the New York and Erie was itself but a portion—a system which, if it shall be completed, will be among the grandest physical achievements of the age. But great as that interest has been, and still is, in its success, I cannot afford to carve out four years of my life as barren of results to myself. The claim I am prosecuting is just. And be the consequences to others, or to the great enterprise itself, what they may, duty to myself requires that it should not be abandoned.

SAMUEL HALLETT.

www.ingramcontent.com/pod-product-compliance
Lightning Source LLC
LaVergne TN
LVHW011138110826
845150LV00008B/2400

* 9 7 8 1 4 1 8 1 9 3 2 8 7 *